Light

by Becky Olien

Consultant:
Philip W. Hammer, Ph.D.
Vice President, The Franklin Center
The Franklin Institute Science Museum

Bridgestone Books
an imprint of Capstone Press
Mankato, Minnesota

Bridgestone Books are published by Capstone Press
151 Good Counsel Drive, P.O. Box 669, Mankato, Minnesota 56002
http://www.capstone-press.com

Library of Congress Cataloging-in-Publication Data
Olien, Rebecca.
    Light / by Becky Olien.
    p. cm.—(Our physical world)
    Includes bibliographical references and index.
    Summary: Introduces light, and provides instructions for an activity to demonstrate
some of its characteristics.
    ISBN 0-7368-1405-1 (hardcover)
    1. Light—Juvenile literature. [1. Light.] I. Title. II. Series.
QC360 .O45 2003
535—dc21   2001007887

Editorial Credits
Erika Mikkelson, editor; Karen Risch, product planning editor; Linda Clavel, designer;
    Anne McMullen, illustrator; Alta Schaffer, photo researcher

Photo Credits
Capstone Press/Jim Foell, 7 (left)
CORBIS, 17
ImageState, Inc., 11
PhotoDisc, Inc., cover
Photri-Microstock, 7 (right); L.L. Rue, 15
The Stock Market/Michael Keller, 21
Tom Till, 9
Visuals Unlimited/Gene Rhoden, 5; Patrick J. Endres, 13; Tom Uhlman, 19

1 2 3 4 5 6 07 06 05 04 03 02

Table of Contents

Light. 4

Light Travels 6

Light Reflects. 8

Light Bends 10

Color. 12

Plants Need Light 14

Thomas Edison 16

Using Light 18

Safety 20

Hands On: Making Shadows 22

Words to Know 23

Read More 23

Internet Sites 24

Index. 24

Light

Light is a form of energy. Energy gives objects the ability to move or do work. Most sources of heat also give off light. The Sun is a huge ball of burning gas that gives off light. The Sun shines light on Earth. Lightning also gives off light.

Light Travels

Light travels in a straight line unless an object is in its way. Opaque (oh-PAKE) objects block light and form shadows. Trees and people are opaque. Light travels through transparent objects. Windows and eyeglasses are transparent.

opaque
not letting light through

Light Reflects

People see light that reflects off objects. Light best reflects off white or shiny objects. Light can reflect off water. The Moon does not make its own light. It reflects light from the Sun.

reflect
to return light
from an object

8

TRY THIS

Fill a pan with water. Place the pan near a wall. Turn off the lights. Shine a flashlight on the water. Hold the flashlight at different angles. Does the light reflect off the water and onto the wall?

9

Light Bends

Light slows when moving through transparent objects. Light bends when it changes speed. Bending light is called refraction. Lenses refract light. Lenses can be made of curved glass or plastic. Lenses help people see in new ways. Magnifying glasses and eyeglasses use lenses.

Eyes are lenses. They sometimes do not bend light enough to see clearly. Eyeglasses refract light to help people see better.

Color

Light from the Sun is called white light. Bending light separates white light into different colors. A prism refracts light.

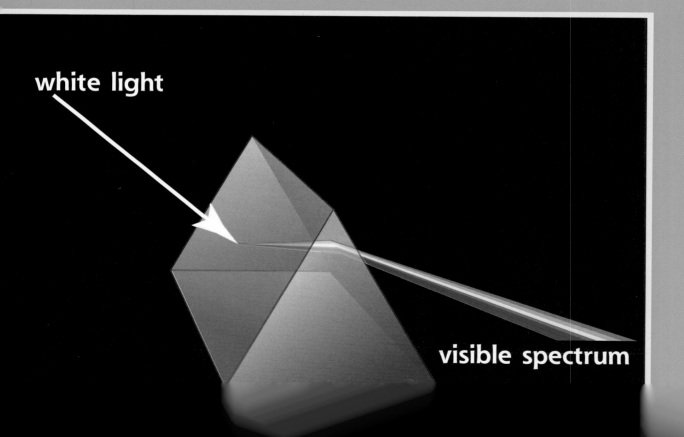

white light

visible spectrum

Light traveling through a prism separates into different colors to make a rainbow. These colors make up the visible spectrum.

visible spectrum

the colors we see when light shines through a prism

Plants Need Light

Plants use the energy from light to make food. Green leaves and stems soak in sunlight. Plants use light to change water and air into food. Plants use food for energy to live and grow. Plants cannot live without light.

Thomas Edison

In 1879, Thomas Edison invented the lightbulb. Thomas used electricity to heat a piece of thread. The heated thread glowed inside a glass bulb. People used candles and oil lanterns before the lightbulb was invented.

electricity
a form of energy

Inventing the lightbulb was not easy. Thomas Edison tried thousands of times before a lightbulb stayed lit for a long period of time. The first lightbulb that worked well lasted 40 hours.

Using Light

Light has many uses. Farmers need light for their crops to grow. Light from the Sun can be made into electricity using solar panels. Lasers are narrow light beams. Doctors use lasers to perform operations. Machines use lasers to scan price codes, play compact discs, and cut metal.

solar panel

19

Safety

Eyes use light to see. The pupil is a hole that lets light into the eye. Too much light can harm the eye.

Your pupil gets bigger in less light. More light can enter your eye.

pupil

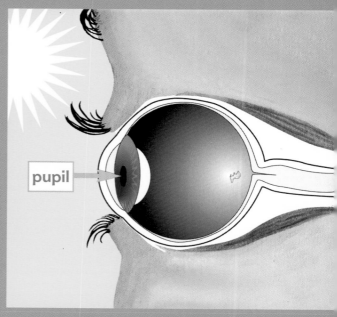

pupil

Your pupil gets smaller in bright light. Less light enters your eye.

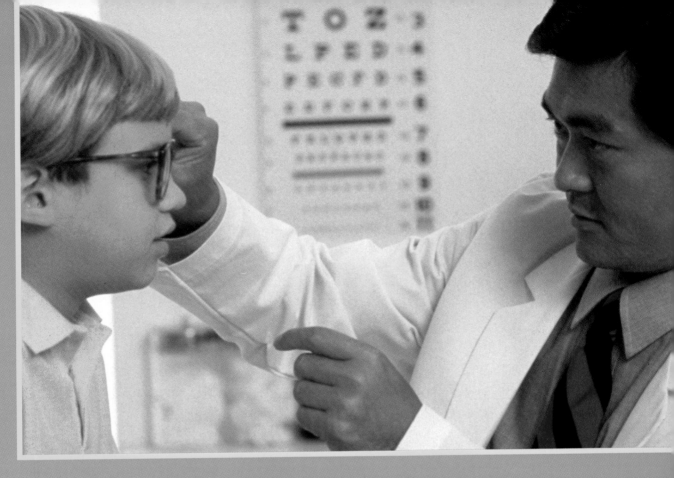

Never look directly at the Sun. Do not put
sharp objects near your eyes. Have your
eyes checked regularly by a doctor.

Hands On: Making Shadows

This activity will show you how to change the shadow of a toy.

What You Need

Small plastic toy
Piece of white paper
Flashlight

What You Do

1. Place the plastic toy on a piece of white paper.
2. Shine the flashlight at the toy. Do you see a shadow?
3. Hold the flashlight close to the toy. How does the shadow look?
4. Move the flashlight farther away. How does the shadow change?
5. Hold the flashlight so it shines straight down on top of the toy. Can you still see a shadow?
6. Watch the shadow as you move the flashlight down toward the paper. The toy's shadow should get longer.

The toy has a shadow because light travels in a straight line. The toy blocks light from hitting the paper. Shadows change size depending on the direction of the light. Shadows are longest when the light is held low.

Words to Know

energy (EN-ur-jee)—the ability to move things or do work; light is a form of energy.

invent (in-VENT)—to think of and make something new; Thomas Edison invented the lightbulb.

prism (PRIZ-uhm)—a transparent, triangle-shaped plastic or glass object that bends light

pupil (PYOO-puhl)—the round, black center of your eye that lets light travel through it

reflect (ri-FLEKT)—to return light from an object

refraction (ri-FRAKT-shun)—the bending of light; light is refracted when it travels through a prism or a lens.

transparent (transs-PAIR-uhnt)—letting light through

Read More

Berger, Samantha. *Light.* Science Emergent Readers. New York: Scholastic, 1999.

Hidalgo, Maria. *Light.* Let's Investigate. Mankato, Minn.: Creative Education, 2002.

Miller-Schroeder, Patricia. *The Science of Light & Color.* Living Science. Milwaukee: Gareth Stevens, 2000.

Internet Sites

BrainPOP—Light
http://www.brainpop.com/science/light/light/index
Edison Kids: Energy Heroes—Thomas Edison
http://www.edisonkids.com/heroexb/thomas.htm

Index

Edison, Thomas, 16, 17
electricity, 16, 18
energy, 4, 14
heat, 4
lasers, 18
lenses, 10, 11
lightbulb, 16, 17
Moon, 8
opaque, 6
plants, 14

prism, 12, 13
pupil, 20
rainbow, 13
reflect, 8, 9
refraction, 10, 11, 12
shadows, 6
Sun, 4, 8, 12, 18, 21
sunlight, 13, 14
transparent, 6, 10
visible spectrum, 13